PURA'S CUENTOS

How Pura Belpré
Reshaped Libraries
with Her Stories

written by Annette Bay Pimentel
illustrated by Magaly Morales

Abrams Books for Young Readers
New York

Pura Belpré needs stories like a mango tree needs sunshine,
like a coquí frog needs green leaves.
Abuela always has a story.
She tells Pura about beautiful Martina.
She crows in the voice of Señor Gallo

¡QUI-QUI-RI-QUI!

¡MIAU, MIAU!

BOROM·BOROM

and quacks for Señor Pato.

    She tells how Pérez bows low
and asks Martina to marry him.

    Pura giggles . . . shivers . . . sighs.
She drinks up Abuela's cuentos.

¡CUAC!

¿SE QUIERE CASAR CONMIGO?

When she is grown, Pura feels
the tug of family who have moved
far away from Puerto Rico.
So she boards a ship.
¡Adiós!

In New York City, she misses the taste
of mango and the call of the coquí.
She misses Abuela's cuentos.
But Harlem bubbles with its own exciting stories.
It thrums with dancing feet and swirling satin.
Drums rumble. Saxophones wail.

In the hush of the 135th Street branch library, Pura sees shelves and shelves of stories. She watches a librarian pull a book from the shelf, hand it to a girl.

She thinks, *If I could do what that lady is doing for the rest of my life, I would be the happiest person on earth.*

Pura shops, runs errands in the
neighborhood, maybe stops to tap her toe
to trumpet riffs. The librarian watches
Pura chat with Spanish speakers the
librarian can't understand, hears her slide
from Sí to Yes with English speakers.

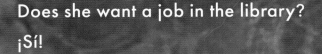

Does she want a job in the library?
¡Sí!
Pura reads the books in the children's
section. Stories from Ireland. From
Germany. From Italy. But where is
Puerto Rico? Where are Señor Gallo,
Señor Pato, Pérez and Martina? Why aren't
Abuela's stories on these shelves?

Pura is put in charge of storytime. Here in the library there are rules, even for storytellers.

Light the candle.

Open the book.

Tell the story.

Oh, Pura can tell a story! She hisses . . . murmurs . . . roars.
Children lean forward. They giggle . . . shiver . . . sigh.

She is allowed to tell only stories that have been printed in a
book. That's the rule. So she always tells strangers' stories.

But Pura knows that not all the stories worth telling are in
books. She wants to make children giggle at silly Señor Gallo and
cry over Pérez the mouse. She wants to tell Abuela's stories!

Pura decides: She will break the rule.

¡ES UN DÍA PRECIOSO!

She works on crowing like Señor Gallo,
"¡Qui-qui-ri-quí!" Booming like Señor Zapo,
"¡Borom! ¡Borom!" She practices grand gestures
to suggest Pérez's fine plumed hat and hums
sad melodies for Martina's mournful song. Every
word, every action breathes life into the story.

¡QUI-QUI-RI-QUÍ!

It's Pura's turn to tell a story for her bosses.
She has watched the other librarians. They light the candle,
show the book, read about courageous kings and beautiful
queens. She has a different plan: She will tell about a
cockroach who falls in love with a mouse.

She is going to tell Abuela's story.

¡BOROM!

Do her hands shake?

Maybe. But still, she lights the candle. When she turns
to face the listeners, her hands are empty.

No book?!

"There once lived a Spanish cockroach called Martina."
Pura tells Abuela's story just as she has practiced.

"The mouse squeaked, 'Chui, chui.'" The audience giggles.

"Pretty Martina, will you marry me?" Everyone sighs.

"He lost his balance and fell into the kettle."
Shivers and groans.

Everyone knows Pura has broken the rule:
Her story is not in any book on any library shelf.
But . . .

YES, I WILL MARRY YOU!

. . . what a story!

"Thanks, Miss Belpré," one of the bosses smiles. "I am a little tired of kings and queens."

It is decided: Pura may tell her own story, as long as she says that someday it may be made into a book.

Children whose families come from Ireland, Germany, Italy, from other parts of the United States—they all flock to the libraries where Pura tells stories. They drink up Pura's stories, so new to them. But where are the children whose families already know about Pérez and Martina? Where are the children from Puerto Rico? From Venezuela? From Mexico?

Walking the neighborhood,
Pura finds them.

LIMONADA POR FAVOR

¡PERDÓN!

¡CU

¡ME TOCA A MÍ!

But she does not see them in the library.
Pura wants to tell stories to these children, too.
So she spreads the word.

Children new to the city, new to English,
come to the library.
Pura lights the candle.
She tells los cuentos. En español.
Some from books. Some not.

CUEN

¡GRACIAS!

¡ELLA HABLA ESPAÑOL!

TOS

Pura fills the heads of the children with stories, their arms with books. Gracias, they say as they leave the library. They will be back. This library is their library now.

LA MARIPOSA
MONARCA

¡NOS CONTÓ HISTORIAS DE PUERTO RICO!

As the years go by, Pura continues telling her stories, sometimes in English, sometimes en español.

Sometimes she tells them to children crowded into library corners. Sometimes she tells them to students spread across huge auditoriums.

She helps children act out the stories and tell them with puppets.

Pura's stories become their stories. Even though those stories are still not in books.

They *should* be in books!

Pura scribbles, scratches out, erases, and begins again.

It's hard to get Abuela's stories just right on the page.

But one day when Pura reads what she
has written, she tastes the tang of mango,
hears the call of the coquí. "Many years ago in
a little house with a round balcony, there once
lived a Spanish cockroach called Martina.
She was a pretty cockroach with black eyes
and soft brown skin . . ."

Ah! Finally right.

Abuela's story . . . Pura's story . . .
the children's story . . . becomes a book.
Because Pura Belpré always knew that
many stories worth telling aren't in books.

Not yet.

AUTHOR'S NOTE

Your story will not happen on paper; it will happen first in the imagination of your reader.
—Pura Belpré

Pura Belpré grew up in Puerto Rico in a family of "natural storytellers." She recalled "sucking sugar cane or eating mangoes" while listening to her father's stories and hearing many folktales from her grandmother. She loved wandering the countryside "listening to the wind and watching the awakening of the living creatures," many of which later appeared in her stories.

In 1920, she moved to New York City. She lived just steps from the Apollo Theater and other famous jazz venues during the Harlem Renaissance. We have no record of how often she tapped her toes to jazz or peeked through doors at swing dancers. But we do know that in her job at the 135th Street branch library (today the Schomburg Center for Research in Black Culture), she witnessed a cultural outpouring. "I experienced the Black Renaissance of art and literature, and the upsurge of Poets, Novelists, Dramatists and Musicians." The work she was so passionate about—bringing Puerto Rico into the library—was informed by this larger movement to honor and preserve the stories and experiences of marginalized people.

As a new library employee, Belpré attended classes at the New York Public Library Training School. It was in her storytelling class that she first decided to try to reshape library policy. She took an audacious risk as a low-level staffer defying the rule that all stories had to be from published sources. Happily, her storytelling dazzled supervisors, and an exception was carved out for her: She was allowed to tell children stories that didn't come from books.

I am personally especially indebted to Belpré for her brilliant idea of offering bilingual storytimes. She was the first New York librarian to offer stories in more than one language—and perhaps the first in the country. When our family lived in Bosnia, my kindergartener came home from her local Bosnian school sadder and sadder every day. It was a bilingual storytime that finally helped her connect to the other kindergarteners and made her feel like their school was her school. The bilingual storytime movement, sparked by Belpré, has helped many families like mine feel welcome in new places.

Belpré had a great rapport with children. At one branch, concerned that the library only had clubs for girls, she started a boys' puppet club. She taught the boys how to sculpt heads and sew clothing for puppets, as well as how to select and present plays. On a marionette controller, one of the boys, Harry Burnett, signed his name, and above his name, all in caps, he wrote the name of the librarian he obviously adored: "PURA BELPRÉ."

Belpré published *Perez and Martina* as a picture book in 1932. After she retired from the library in 1943, she published individual and collected Puerto Rican folktales as well as original contemporary stories. She also translated many popular English language picture books into Spanish. In the 1960s, she returned to the library to work on the South Bronx Project, where she helped develop a bibliography of Spanish-language books so libraries everywhere could improve their Spanish-language collections. And, a "natural storyteller" like the rest of her family, she continued visiting libraries and schools to delight children with cuentos.

She died in 1982, the day after receiving the Mayor's Award for Arts and Culture.

Today Belpré's love of story and community is commemorated in the Pura Belpré Award, given every year to the Latinx illustrator and author whose works best portray, affirm, and celebrate the Latinx experience.

NOTES

p. 2 "¡Qui-qui-ri-quí!": Belpré, *Pérez y Martina*, 15.

p. 3 "Borom. Borom.": Belpré, *Pérez y Martina*, 35.

p. 3 "¿Se quiere casar conmigo?": Belpré, *Pérez y Martina*, 39.

p. 6 "If I could do . . .": Hernández-Delgado, "Pura Teresa Belpré," 428.

p. 12 Señor Zapo: In the Spanish version of her book, Belpré named this character Señor Zapo, which sounds similar to the word for toad, sapo. But in the English version, she calls him "Señor Frog." I have kept his Spanish name, and in the illustrations he is depicted as a coquí frog, the beloved symbol of Puerto Rico.

p. 14 "There once lived . . .": Belpré, "Perez and Martina," in *The Stories I Read to the Children*, 77.

p. 14 "The mouse squeaked . . .": Belpré, "Perez and Martina," 80.

p. 14 "Pretty Martina . . .": Belpré, "Perez and Martina," 78.

p. 14 "He lost his balance . . .": Belpré, "Perez and Martina," 80.

p. 16 "Thanks, Miss Belpré": Belpré, *The Stories I Read to the Children*, 220.

p. 25 "Many years ago . . .": Belpré, "Perez and Martina," 77.

p. 28 "Your story will not . . .": Belpré, *The Stories I Read to the Children*, 212.

p. 28 "Natural storytellers": Jiménez-García, "Pura Belpré, Lights the Storyteller's Candle," 124.

p. 28 "sucking sugar . . .": Handwritten manuscript in the Pura Belpré Papers.

p. 28 "listening to the wind . . .": Typescript in the Belpré Papers.

p. 28 "I experienced the Black Renaissance . . .": Nuñez, "Remembering Pura Belpré's Early Career at the 135th Street New York Public Library," 63.

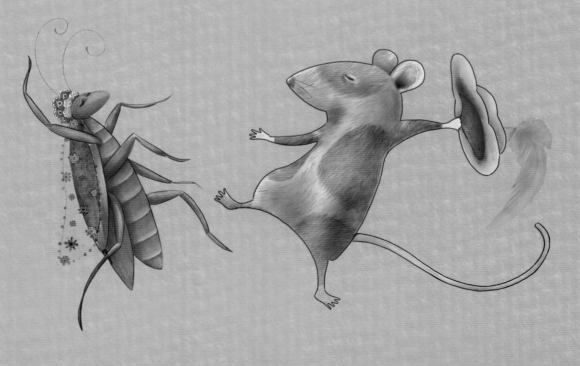

SELECTED BIBLIOGRAPHY

The easiest way to read Pura Belpré's writing today is in the book *The Stories I Read to the Children*, where Lisa Sánchez González has collected many of Belpré's stories, as well as her essays. It's harder to find Belpré's stories in picture book form since most are out of print. You may be able to find them on the shelves of your library or at used bookstores.

Books written by Pura Belpré:

Dance of the Animals. New York: Frederick Warne, 1972.

Firefly Summer. Houston, TX: Piñata Books, 1996.

Juan Bobo and the Queen's Necklace. New York: Frederick Warne, 1962.

Once in Puerto Rico. New York: Frederick Warne, 1973.

Oté. New York: Pantheon Books, 1969.

Perez and Martina. New York: Frederick Warne, 1932.

Perez y Martina. New York: Penguin Group, 2004.

The Rainbow-Colored Horse. New York: Frederick Warne, 1978.

Santiago. New York: Frederick Warne, 1969.

The Tiger and the Rabbit, and Other Tales. Boston: Houghton Mifflin Company, 1946.

Works translated into Spanish by Pura Belpré:

Bonsall, Crosby N. *Caso del forastero hambriento*. New York: Harper, 1969.

Greene, Carla. *Camioneros: ¿Qué hacen?* New York: Harper, 1969.

Hoff, Syd. *Danielito y el dinosauro*. New York: Harper, 1969.

Kessler, Leonard Kessler. *Aquí viene el ponchado*. New York: Harper, 1969.

Leaf, Munro. *El cuento de Ferdinand*. New York: Viking, 1962.

Minarik, Else Holmelund. *Osito*. New York: Harper, 1969.

Newman, Paul. *Ningún lugar para jugar*. New York: Grosset & Dunlap, 1971.

Selsam, Millicent E. *Teresita y las orugas*. New York: Harper, 1969.

Other sources:

To tell this story, I relied heavily on the many essays Belpré wrote about libraries and storytelling. Many have been published, but I also looked at them in manuscript form in the archives of the City University of New York, which has her papers. In their collection, I also got to see and touch some of the exquisite puppets that she made with after-school clubs.

Both Mary K. Conwell, a librarian who worked with Pura Belpré in the 1960s, and Carmen Reyes, a library aide who worked alongside Pura Belpré, generously shared memories of the amazing storyteller and remarkable person Belpré was. They gave me great insight into who she was as a person. Any errors that remain are my own.

Belpré, Pura. *Perez y Martina: Un cuento folklórico puertorriqueño*. New York: Viking, 1991.

Conwell, Mary K. (librarian, New York Public Library). Interview by the author, December 11, 2015.

González, Lisa Sánchez. "Pura Belpré: The Children's Ambassador." *In Latina Legacies: Identity, Biography, and Community*, 148–157. Oxford: Oxford University Press, 2005.

González, Lisa Sánchez. *The Stories I Read to the Children: The Life and Writing of Pura Belpré, the Legendary Storyteller, Children's Author, and New York Public Librarian*. New York: Center for Puerto Rican Studies, 2013.

Hernández-Delgado, Julio L. "Pura Teresa Belpré: Storyteller and Pioneer Puerto Rican Librarian." *The Library Quarterly 62*, no. 4 (October 1992): 425–440.

Jiménez-García, Marilisa. "Pura Belpré Lights the Storyteller's Candle: Reframing the Legacy and What it Means for the Field of Latino/a Studies and Children's Literature." *Centro Journal 26*, no. 1 (2014): 110–147. Online tinyurl.com/s9nxqy7.

López, Lillian, and Pura Belpré. "Reminiscences of Two Turned-on Librarians." In *Puerto Rican Perspectives*, edited by Edward Mapp, 83–96. Metuchen, NJ: The Scarecrow Press, 1974.

Nuñez, Victoria. "Remembering Pura Belpré's Early Career at the 135th Street New York Public Library: Interracial Cooperation and Puerto Rican Settlement During the Harlem Renaissance." *Centro Journal* 21, no. 1 (2009): 53–77.

The Pura Belpré Papers, archives of the Puerto Rican Diaspora, Centro de Estudios Puertorriqueños, Hunter College, City University of New York. [Manuscripts of her stories and essays and her puppets.]

Reyes, Carmen (library aide, New York Public Library). Interview by the author, August 11, 2016.

To Carmen Reyes
A Carmen Reyes —A.B.P.

To my father, Eligio, and my mother, Eloina, for all the love they have given
me, for the support, for the accompaniment, for the care, and for giving me life.
I love you!
A mi papá Eligio y mi mamá Eloína, por todo el amor que me han dado,
por el apoyo, por el acompañamiento, por los cuidados y por darme la vida.
¡Los amo! —M.M.

The illustrations for this book were made with electronic media
like Procreate and Photoshop.

Cataloging-in-Publication Data has been applied for and may be obtained
from the Library of Congress.

ISBN 978-1-4197-4941-4

Text copyright © 2021 Annette Bay Pimentel
Illustrations copyright © 2021 Magaly Morales
Book design by Brenda Echevarrias Angelilli

Printed and bound in China
10 9 8 7 6 5 4 3 2 1

Abrams Books for Young Readers are available at special discounts when purchased
in quantity for premiums and promotions as well as fundraising or educational use.
Special editions can also be created to specification. For details, contact
specialsales@abramsbooks.com or the address below.

Abrams® is a registered trademark of Harry N. Abrams, Inc.

ABRAMS The Art of Books
195 Broadway, New York, NY 10007
abramsbooks.com